MW00813582

IMAGES
of America

GLOVERSVILLE

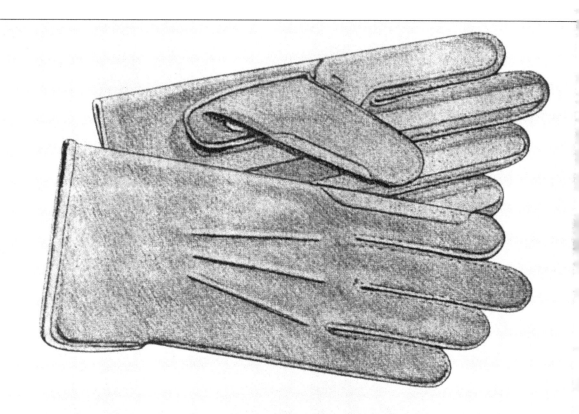

GLOVERSVILLE

GLOVES   AMERICA

In its heyday, Gloversville became the Glove Capital of the nation, if not the world, and at one time, the city's factories produced the most tonnage of leather in the nation. Most every street in the city had a glove or leather factory or some allied industry. It was due to the production of gloves that Gloversville received its name.

IMAGES
of America

GLOVERSVILLE

Lewis G. Decker

ARCADIA
PUBLISHING

Copyright © 1998 by Lewis G. Decker
ISBN 978-1-5316-4193-1

Published by Arcadia Publishing
Charleston, South Carolina

Library of Congress Catalog Card Number: 98-86555

For all general information contact Arcadia Publishing at:
Telephone 843-853-2070
Fax 843-853-0044
E-mail sales@arcadiapublishing.com
For customer service and orders:
Toll-Free 1-888-313-2665

Visit us on the Internet at www.arcadiapublishing.com

These glove machine operators were photographed in Gloversville.

CONTENTS

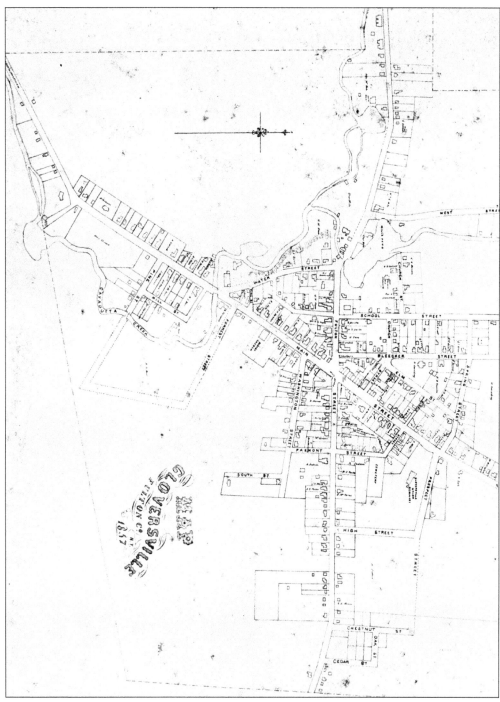

Gloversville, NY, is shown here in 1857.

INTRODUCTION

The city of Gloversville is, and has always been, unique. It is the largest community in Fulton County, with nearly double the population of Johnstown, its twin city, and has always been the industrial might in the county. Most cities are formed from a center nucleus, expanding outward—Johnstown, for example, was planned with surveyors who laid out streets in a north-south and east-west direction, establishing a grid pattern. Gloversville, on the other hand, did the opposite. In the beginning, little attention was paid to planning the city. It grew from three small settlements on the outside and finally merged into a center of what is today the Four Corners in the heart of the city, where North and South Main Streets meet with East and West Fulton Streets. It has streets dissecting and angling one another and running in all directions, and it was not until later years that more orderly patterns of laying out streets were employed.

Of the three outside settlements from which the city emerged, one of the oldest seems to have been what was first called "The Settlement." Later references give it the name of the "Mills Settlement" and "McNab Mills." This was located to the west of the present-day city of Gloversville, down West Fulton Street, and it included what many knew as West Mill Pond. This early settlement was reached from a narrow dirt road leading from Johnstown. A small stream near the intersection of West Fulton Street (Route #29A leading north to Caroga) and Rose Street was dammed up and afforded water power for some of the area's first industries. The small dam was later replaced with a larger one, which in recent years was destroyed, draining the mill pond. This early settlement was where the first minister for the Kingsboro Church was given a residence. It was also here that the Mann Brothers established and manufactured axes (founding what is believed to be the forerunner of the American Axe Company). Here, too, resided the widow Gregg; her husband was the noted Captain Gregg, who, after having been scalped and left for dead during the Revolutionary War, was saved by his dog. The incident was known to area schoolchildren of the early 1800s, as it was written up and used in their childhood primers (it was titled "The Faithful American Dog").

The settlement itself extended down West Fulton Street. It harbored one of the city's first schools, a few doors west of Orchard Street on the north side, located on a small knoll. At one time, just past West Street, at the intersection of West and West Fulton Streets, the Mills brothers established homes across from each other and conducted a series of businesses, damning up the Cayadutta Creek near here. One home is still standing; it later became the headquarters of the German Concordia Club, and is today a tavern. Across the street, the other brother had a large home with a pond beside it; this pond was located on the site of our current city hall. It is told that Mr. Mills enjoyed the delicacy of frog legs and raised bull frogs in his pond. The home was eventually destroyed, and the Fonda, Johnstown and Gloversville Railroad Headquarters and waiting rooms were built on its site (today, a city park is located there). Just below this location, south on the Cayadutta Creek, Philo Mills established his sawmill.

North of the present-day city of Gloversville was located the Kingsboro Settlement. This settlement emerged shortly after the Revolutionary War and was comprised of a number of New England settlers, many of who had served their country during the war. The first church in the area was established here, along with another one of the city's earliest schools. The church was formed by 1793 as a Congregational church, but shortly after was taken over by a Presbyterian congregation. The small settlement grew until, at one period in the city's history, it was thought it would engulf what is today our city of Gloversville. It became a prosperous and close-knit community, with much of its activity revolving around its church. Its minister, Dr. Elisha Yale, was a major influence in this community and has been recognized with a life-like statue in the city park. An academy for higher learning was eventually established here, and many of its residents became the forerunners of the city's early business and professional men. In later years the academy became the site of one of the public schools; today it houses the Fulton County Museum.

The Kingsboro Settlement derived its name from the old Kingsborough patent of Sir William Johnson. In the early 1800s the settlement grew in population and eventually engulfed its neighbors to the south, then nicknamed "Stump City." A large portion of the settlement's land was owned by only a few individuals. One of these men was Mr. Potter, nicknamed "King Potter," who received top dollar for his lots. The small settlement developing at Stump City, along the Cayadutta Creek, was offering cheaper land, especially for the working class, who were migrating there at that time, along with their trades and leather-working abilities. The community and its population grew with the growth of the industries along the creek down in the valley, and enterprising businessmen were attracted here to supply the needs of these workers. Eventually, the thriving settlement of Kingsboro was engulfed by the increasing settlement to the south.

The third settlement that eventually made up the city of Gloversville was originally comprised of a small cluster of homes with a tavern on the hill, where today Kingsboro Avenue intersects with East Fulton Street. The Prospect Hill Cemetery is located on one of these corners today. This little settlement is referred to in early references as the "Settlement on the Hill." Professor Horace Sprague speaks of a Mr. Bedford keeping a tavern at this location. Horace Sprague wrote a small booklet on the history of Gloversville in 1859 titled "Gloversville or the Model Village," making it one of the earliest history of the city of Gloversville. In this history, Mr. Sprague tells of the Throop family moving here as early settlers and notes that this is where Enos T. Throop, later governor of the state of New York, was born. A member of the Throop family is also mentioned as being one of the first burials in the old cemetery at Kingsboro.

It was from these three settlements, which drifted toward the Four Corners, that Gloversville was formed. Just a few years ago in 1990, Gloversville celebrated its 100th anniversary as a chartered city. As early as 1816, Johnathan Sedwik had proposed calling the hamlet "Stump City," because of the number of stumps that had to be removed and pulled up (many were used for stump fences). One of these last stump fences in the city bordered the Mills's property and pond. The settlement bore the nickname Stump City until 1828 when, with the establishment of a post office, it was thought advisable to designate it by a more euphonious name and accordingly, at the suggestion of Jennison Giles and Henry Churchill, it was changed to Gloversville. (Henry Churchill became the first postmaster, officially, on January 29th, 1829.) The name was derived from the great number of gloves that were manufactured in the city.

A number of the settlers who settled here shortly after the American Revolution brought with them their trades, one of which was tinsmithing. Those who settled in the Kingsborough settlement and north on Easterly and Phelps Streets were especially skilled in tinsmithing. In addition to producing tin-ware, they peddled their wares across the country. A lot of bartering for goods took place (exchanging goods for goods), and on occasion these peddlers brought back deer and animal hides from their northern excursions. Using their New England ingenuity, they used these hides as a source of income, making them into gloves, a much-needed commodity in those early days—especially during our winter months, for workers on the farm and for teamsters driving wagons. The gloves became a popular item and emerged into a cottage industry, which eventually involved most of the families in the area. Patterns were traced in the furs and and then hand-sewn together. Two local men, Ezekiel Case of Kingsborough and Tallamage Edwards of Johnstown, are credited with introducing ways to process leather faster, to better take advantage of the demand for gloves. When a wagonload of gloves was taken to Boston, the gloves were met with great demand, and from that time on, leather processing and glove making became the major industry in this locality.

Eventually, with the coming of the railroad, the city and its inhabitants were opened up to the outside world. Gloversville became known in its hey-day as the "Glove Capital of the World;" at one time it produced the most tonnage of leather in the nation. Gone now are the trains and the large railroad station that once bustled with workers and commerce in the large freight yards. Gone too are the large crowds waiting to board a train to "the Coney Island of the north," on its northern run to Sacandaga Park. The waiting rooms and depot have disappeared along with the shoe-shine stand and spacious benches. The city and county are planning to use the old railroad bed for a lineal park through the two cities, with a bike and hiking trail. At present there is a movement to establish a railroad museum in the city of Gloversville to help preserve the memory of the old F.J.& G. Railroad.

The center of the city, what we now refer to as the Four Corners, is the intersection of North and South Main Streets and West and East Fulton Streets. Here the city finally emerges into the business, financial, and entertainment district of Gloversville. At one time almost every street in the city had a glove or leather factory or some business allied with this industry. Main Street was always busy with workers and businessmen patronizing the many restaurants and lunch stands. Pay day was on Fridays and, with everyone working, Main Street was elbow-to-elbow with shoppers on their way home from work. The theaters were kept busy with vaudeville and traveling shows and Gloversville had a reputation of being a circus town, with most of all the main circuses during the season making a stop here. Gloversville was noted to have survived the Depression with ample work and it advertised that a man could find an industrious wife in Gloversville, as it was a haven for employed ladies in the many glove factories.

Gloversville has produced many notable citizens. Many have held high state and county positions, in both politics and industry. Frederick Remington, the famous artist of the west, won the hand of a Gloversville lass and left his mark on the community. In later years, a Polish immigrant of Jewish faith came to Gloversville and later moved to California to become the famous Samuel Goldwyn of MGM fame. Lucius Littauer, a son of an immigrant, resided in Gloversville and eventually attended Harvard, where he became a close friend of Teddy Roosevelt and remained so throughout his life. He became a congressman from our area and a renowned local industrialist, contributing as a benefactor to the city, and has been memorialized with a life-size statue in tribute to him in our city park. A number of public buildings, a playground, a hospital, and streets bear his name. The city can boast of many fine actors, actresses, and entertainers in its past; famous in their own right, they journeyed here to perform on the stages of the old Darling and the Kasson Opera House, which later became the Family Theater. At one time Gloversville was the headquarters of the famous Schine Enterprise, known across the nation for entertainment and hotels. They had some of the first and finest movies of the day show here. The city at one period had its own movie studio, called The Blaze Studio, located on old Elm Street. Today the city is trying to restore its old Glove Theater with a group of dedicated local individuals and once again bring back the arts and entertainment to the area.

Gloversville's many old churches and its synagogue still call their congregations to service, some with their high steeples reaching to the heavens, adding to the city's skyline. Today the Arterial Highway, State Highway 30A, bypasses the city to the east, heading north. The city no longer boasts of a hotel; the old Kingsborough Hotel, an impressive building, is the last remnant of this era. Closed for years, it was once one of the city's centers of activity. It served as an arena for eating, lodging, and congregating. Recently the old structure was restored and made into apartments. The city's new high-rise for the elderly presents a new view to the city's skyline. The old city hall on Main Street now serves as a restaurant; a new city hall has replaced it on Frontage Road, serving as a combined fire and emergency building. The old high school on Main Street is now used as a administration building for the school system. A new high school was built on Lincoln Street, overlooking the city; only recently the Estee School (the Gloversville Middle School) has been rebuilt next to the high school on the hill.

Gloversville is trying to bring back its old glory; organizations, city government, and dedicated individuals are working on ways to improve its image. The Fulton County Regional Chamber of Commerce and Industry, headquartered in Gloversville, and groups like SPRING (Society to Promote and Revitalize in Gloversville) are trying to help accomplish this. Gloversville still maintains its local newspaper (the *Leader Herald*), a radio station, and a newly established television station. It has a proud past and promising future.

In this publication I would like to share with you some of Gloversville's glory days through photographs of old scenes, buildings, and events. Reminisce with me in Gloversville's past history.

Lewis G. Decker
Gloversville, N.Y.

One

THE THREE SETTLEMENTS

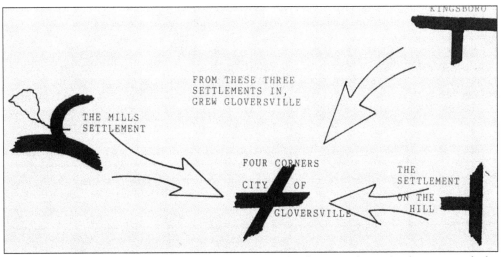

It was from the Settlement (the Mills Settlement), the Kingsboro Settlement, and the Settlement on the Hill that the present-day city of Gloversville emerged.

"The Settlement," later called "the Mills Settlement" and also called "McNab's Mills," is believed to have started at the crossroads of what is today Rose Street and the extension of West Fulton, where a small stream crosses. It was here that the stream was dammed up to provide waterpower for some of the area's first industries. The small dam pictured here was later enlarged, and the body of water became known as the West Mill Pond. The widow Gregg's home can be seen in the center of this picture. This home, before it was removed and the pond enlarged to back up the waters of the West Mill Pond, had fallen into a dilapidated condition and became known as "the haunted house" (it was a favorite place for spiritualist groups to hold seances). This is one of the earliest photographs of the city, taken from an old daguerreotype.

This is a much later view of the West Mill Pond, with the tanned hides in the background laid out to dry and bleach. This was an early phase in the old method of processing manufactured leather.

The West Mill Pond was dammed up, and its clear water afforded water power for the settlement's early industries. When frozen in the winter, it produced cakes of ice for residents of the village, and later the city of Gloversville. Remember when we had to empty the pan under the ice box of its melted ice and how children used to follow the ice wagon on a hot summer day for a sliver of ice to suck on?

This is Mr. Darling of Bleecker Street, one of the city's last ice dealers, delivering ice. Electric refrigerators replaced the old ice boxes and the cards that used to be placed in the window, telling the ice man how many pounds were needed that day.

One of Gloversville's oldest schools was located on West Fulton Street, just west of what is today Orchard Street. The old Spring Street School served the west end section of the city until the present-day McNab School was built. The school's site on Spring Street has been converted into a city park and playground, extending from Spring Street to Cherry Street.

The John McNab home in the west end of the city was part of this early settlement. McNab, a Scotsman, established his mills in this section and later built this elaborate home. It is told he wanted nothing but the best materials in its construction and even had the white sands of one of our northern lakes used in the mixing of the plaster.

Mr. McNab, in his later years, took ill and went to the medicine cabinet to procure some medicine in a bottle; in the dark he mistakenly drank from a poison bottle. The present-day McNab School occupies this site today.

The Charles Mills Sr. home was located on West Fulton Street on the east side of the intersection of West Street. This old home was later torn down to make room for the new Fonda, Johnstown and Gloversville Railroad Station. Mr. Mills's pond was to the northeast of his home, where he had dammed up the Cayadutta Creek. Mr. Mills is said to have liked frog legs as a delicacy and raised bull frogs in his pond. On one side of this pond remained one of the last stump fences in the city, contributing to the nickname Stump City. The pond was later filled in, and is today the site of the new city hall. Members of the Mills family were early settlers and a prominent family in Gloversville. This home was believed to be built in 1830; the picture was taken in the early 1870s.

The F.J. & G.R.R. waiting station and offices, built in the 1870s on the site of Charles Mills Sr. home, can be seen here in the background. This picture shows one of Gloversville's first soft ice cream stands, across from the present-day "Choo Choo's" ice cream stand. A Dairy Queen, operated by Earl Hoag, later moved to become the "Idle Hour" on the Arterial Highway. Today this is part of the Railroad Park's parking lot.

This residence, on the northwest corner of West and West Fulton Streets, was built by one of the Mills brothers. The other brother built his home on the opposite corner, where the F.J. & G.R.R. waiting station and offices were later built. Later this home became the headquarters of the German Concordia Club (organized in 1899); today it houses a local tavern called "The Cellar." The horse-drawn delivery wagon in the foreground belonged to Berghoff's Market, across the street.

Mr. Berghoff's market is shown here on West Fulton Street, across from West Street; next door was the Seaboard Shellfish Company. To the left of the photo can be seen part of the Fulton Hotel; today C.J.'s Electrical Supply occupies the spot.

This is William Jennings Bryan on a whistle stop to Gloversville while campaigning for the presidency. The Hotel Fulton can be seen in the background on West Fulton Street.

Ringling Brothers and Barnum and Bailey unload from a train, July 11, 1931, on West Fulton Street. The rail yards can be seen in the background, along with the freight station and coal barn.

This is an interior view of the F.J. & G.R.R. repair shop, located off West Fulton Street. The local railroad had its own facilities for repairs and built some of its own cars here.

One of the F.J. & G. R.R.'s early steam engines, the "David A. Wells," is shown here with its crew at the train yards.

FULTON COUNTY

SITE OF
THE HEADQUARTERS OF THE
FONDA, JOHNSTOWN AND
GLOVERSVILLE, RAIL ROAD
1870-1984
FULTON COUNTY
HISTORIAN 1995

This historic marker, off West Fulton Street, is in the new city park. Also in the park is a 50-foot metal boxcar. It is being refurbished and efforts are being made to convert it into a railroad museum, housing memorabilia of the old F.J. & G.R.R. The old track has been torn up and there is a movement on to make the old railroad bed between the two cities, Gloversville and Johnstown, into a lineal park for bicycling and hiking.

The Kingsboro Settlement became so prosperous it was considered, at one time, to have been the leading settlement; today it remains one of the most historic in our city. A bronze plaque depicting the area's early settlement, showing the original location of the church, school, and early homes, has been placed on a natural glacial boulder at the head of the park, at what is believed to be the former site of a watering trough for horses.

In this park is located, on the site of the original church, this monument erected in honor of Dr. Elisha Yale, pastor of the old Kingsboro Church. In addition he organized The "Kingsboro Academy." He was one of Kingsboro's and the city of Gloversville's most respected and prominent citizens of his day.

The original old Kingsboro Church was organized in 1793 and occupied a location in the present-day park. Later, in the 1850s, the church shown here was built to replace it. Today this park represents a typical New England town common, although it was not planned as such originally. The original church was Congregational; later, during Dr. Yale's period, it became Presbyterian. Today it houses the Glove Cities Assembly of God.

This is an artist's sketch and interpretation of the original church (1793) that stood in the present-day Kingsboro Park. Note the old schoolhouse in the background, next to the cemetery.

22

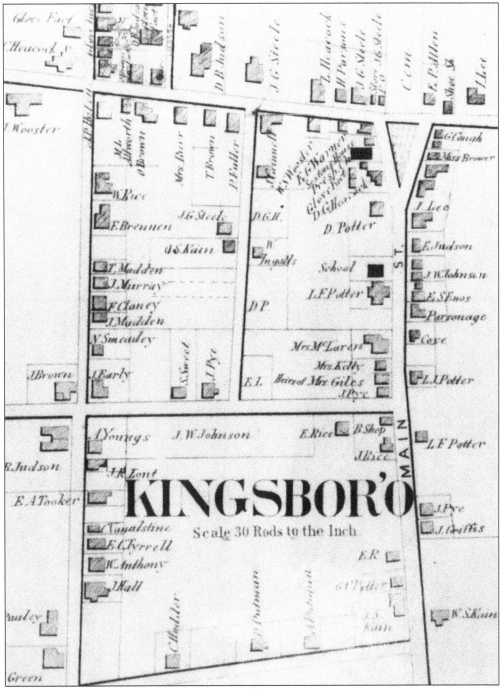

This early map of Kingsboro Settlement is dated 1868.

The old Kingsboro Academy in the Kingsboro section of Gloversville is today the site of the Fulton County Museum. The date of the old academy is inscribed with colored brick on the rear entrance, and on the front entrance of the museum is the date the present building was built as part of the city's school system. Many of our city's and county's early prominent residents were educated in this old academy.

This is an early group of students who attended the old Kingsboro School when it was still a wooden structure.

A 1906 parade float depicting the old historic church at Kingsboro is shown here, with schoolchildren dressed as early settlers.

One of the oldest homes in the Kingsboro Park section of the city of Gloversville is the old Allen home. The original settler of the Allen family was believed to have been related to the famous Ethan Allen of Vermont fame. The home has been altered in later years, with a second-story addition. Today this old historic home is owned and occupied by Robyn and Alexander Isabella.

"King Potter's" home, in the old section of Kingsboro, is one of our city's most impressive residences today. Now owned and occupied by Mrs. Ralph O. Collins (Delia), this old home was once a tavern; the barroom portion of the old tavern is used today as a dining room (still featuring its massive exterior door on the north side and its original fireplace). Upstairs was the ballroom.

This old Kingsboro Park home is probably one of the oldest in the park still maintaining its original appearance. It is believed to have been built by Philip Mead, one of the early settlers in this community, and certainly adds to the historic atmosphere of this old section of the city of Gloversville.

This historic marker designates the site of the old academy and is placed in front of the present-day Fulton County Museum, on the corner of Kingsboro Avenue and Academy Place.

An old fountain once occupied the center of the Kingsboro Park until local residents complained of the children wading in it and causing a disturbance in the park. The fountain was later dismantled, but for years part of it graced the front yard of a camp in Caroga Lake, NY.

This is the site of the old Burying Grounds in Kingsboro. The large butternut tree that once occupied its place in the cemetery has long since disappeared and has been replaced with a large impressive bronze statue dedicated to the early pioneers of old Kingsboro. The butternut tree became the Kingsboro settlement's unofficial directory, where young boys carved their initials alongside those of their girlfriends.

This photo shows the old Kingsboro Waiting Station on the F.J. & G.R.R., which ran north from here to Sacandaga Park and Northville and over to Broadalbin. Mr. Smith's old gas station can be seen in the foreground on Kingsboro Avenue. This is now King's Auto and Truck Repair.

Dr. Elisha Yale is shown here in a portrait photograph.

Leaving the Kingsboro Settlement and proceeding south on Kingsboro Avenue, a couple doors south of the Eighth Avenue intersection, is the city's oldest existing home, known as the Burr home. Originally, the land sloped down to the road in front of this structure. When Kingsboro Avenue was widened, the slope was removed, exposing the front of the cellar. Today Dr. Esposito resides here.

This is the location of "The Settlement on the Hill." Near the intersection of what is today East Fulton Street and Kingsboro Avenue was a tavern, kept by a Mr. Bedford, and a few scattered houses. Today this location includes the city's largest cemetery, Prospect Hill Cemetery. This old photo shows the superintendent of the grounds, Thomas Barker, down on one knee in the center with a white beard.

On one of the streets in this location was evidence for years of a sod circle, where the early circuses used to set up and perform. One early incident tells of the loss of a circus wagon and its team—coming down the grade on East Fulton Street, the horses could not check their load and were run over by it. This photo shows a circus wagon in Gloversville. The year was 1902.

Two

DOWNTOWN

This view looks up North Main Street from Gloversville's Four Corners. The buildings on the left of the picture are the wooden structures on the west side of North Main Street before the great fire of 1877. Note the flag pole on the street.

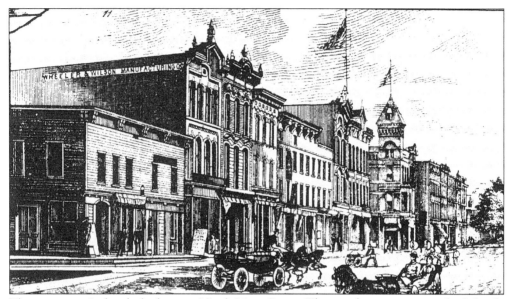

This is an artist's sketch, looking up North Main Street. The wooden structure on the left side of the drawing, on the corner of West Fulton and North Main, was once the site of the city's second school. Today, Van De Walker's jewelry store is located here. This sketch appeared in the *New York Graphic*, October 22, 1879.

This is a later view of this corner of the Rose Block, built in 1881. Note the cigar store Indian called Old Smoke, located on the corner in front of Dailey's Cigar Store. Old Smoke remained vigilant for years, peering down South Main Street.

Note the horse-drawn trolley in this similar view of the C.W. Rose Block at the Four Corners. The Gloversville, Johnstown and Kingsboro horse-drawn trolley remained until electrified and became part of the F.J. & G. R.R. Electric Division.

This is a later view of the northwest corner of the Four Corners. The large window on the second floor to the left of the photo eventually became the headquarters of the city's radio station, WENT, with Joe Tobin. How many remember "Squawker Walker" and his "Pals of the Saddle?"

These two buildings stood a few doors up from the West Fulton and North Main Street intersection; they are well remembered as Cowles and Brown (who also ran a lending library in the rear of the store) and Barney Galinsky and Sons Clothiers. Today this is the vacant lot on Main Street that leads as a shortcut to Bleecker Street.

Gloversville's Four Corners are shown here, looking up North Main Street, with the vacant lot on the northeast corner. Later the Fulton County National Bank was built here. Today it is the Fulton County Regional Chamber of Commerce and Industry Offices. They used to string Japanese lanterns in the trees and put on strawberry festivals in this lot. Gloversville was always ready for a parade.

The Four Corners are shown here, again with the vacant lot to the right on East Fulton Street. The home with the white columns later became the headquarters for the Fulton County Veterans Agency; in recent years it was torn down.

This impressive white marble bank building later occupied the vacant lot as the Fulton County National Bank. Today this structure is the headquarters of the Fulton County Regional Chamber of Commerce and Industry.

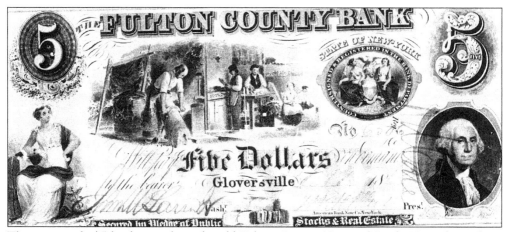

This is an early $5 bank note from the old Fulton County National Bank. Note the etching which depicts the leather and glove making for which the city was noted.

Looking up North Main from the Four Corners, on the east side, the large mansard roof of the Kasson Opera House can be seen in addition to the small wooden structures known as the Marley Block (they were destroyed by fire in March of 1916).

Mr. Marley is in the center of this photograph with a dark moustache, holding a sample of his cigars. To the right of him is a cigar store Indian. Mr. Marley and his son peddled his cigars across the state; note the old stove top hats.

This is the Marley Block fire of March 17, 1916. You might say, "Mr. Marley's cigar store went up in smoke."

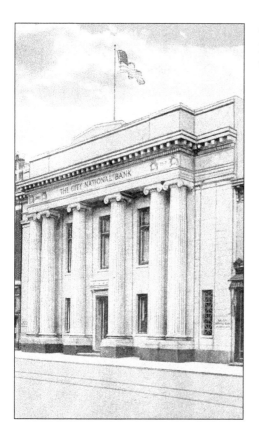

This impressive structure later replaced the Marley Block and is today still maintained as the Gloversville City National Bank.

The southwest side of the Four Corners is shown here. West Fulton Street is on the right in the photo. This corner was a favorite stop for the buses headed to Johnstown and on to Schenectady. The early history of the city tells of large scales located here for livestock feed, hay, and coal.

This is another view of the southwest corners, with one of the horse-drawn trolleys traveling down South Main Street.

Looking down South Main, from the Four Corners in years past, one could always see a traffic policeman directing traffic, both before and after the electric signal lights were installed. Note the police officer in the center of the road with a signal device, which he worked manually, indicating whether to stop or go.

The old Windsor Hotel was one of the city's largest structures and its finest hotel, noted for its lodging and lounge. The brick structure took the place of the old Mills Temperance House that originally occupied these corners. When it was first built it was considered the largest structure this side of Schenectady and Utica. The corner of South Main and East Fulton Streets is shown here; today it is a vacant lot.

This is a later view of the Hotel Windsor on the Four Corners. The Nicholas Coffee Shop used to be on the corner, and south of it was Trask's Cigar Store. The Leader Republican building is to the extreme left, today the home of our *Leader Herald* newspaper.

This is an unusual view of the Four Corners, looking down South Main Street, with five trolley cars at the intersection.

The Four Corners are shown here in the depths of winter. Note the high snowbanks. The Hotel Windsor is in the background.

This view of the east side of South Main Street by the Four Corners shows Avery and Son's Crockery Store. An open trolley car is proceeding up Main Street.

Looking up South Main Street to the Four Corners, a political campaign banner is across Main Street, advertising "The People's Choice"—James G. Blaine and John A. Logan.

This was the "Welcome Home" parade for our veterans returning from the First World War. Marching on South Main Street, they are approaching the Four Corners, April 7, 1919.

Preparing for the homecoming of our doughboys, April 7, 1919, a replica of the Arc de Triomphe was built and placed on North Main Street, just above the Four Corners.

The west side of North Main Street above the Four Corners is shown here. The wooden building to the right of the picture is the original First Methodist Church, on the corner of Church Street and North Main. Later, the church rebuilt its brick edifice in Bleecker Street Square and the old church was used as a furniture store and undertaker establishment by Mr. C.W. Bellows and Son. Church Street was named after this church.

These ruins remained after the great fire on Main Street, May 21, 1877. The foundation in the foreground was the site of Mr. Bellow's store, where the fire started. Sparks flew across Church Street, igniting and burning down all the structures on the west side of North Main from Church Street to Middle Street.

Until this section was rebuilt the same year, it was called the "burnt district." This scene is looking back down North Main Street.

Today, if you walk down the east side of North Main Street, you will observe, across the street between the area of Church and Middle Streets, the dates of 1877 in the eves of the rebuilt buildings.

These are the buildings that replaced the burnt district, still part of North Main Street today. Note the vacant lot to the right of the picture. This is what checked the fire. The wooden house on the corner was the Widow Mills's home. Later torn down, a large three-story building was built here that housed the Darling and Denton Store.

This picture shows the corner of North Main and Church Streets, which, at the time, housed an ice cream parlor. Upstairs, in later years, Mr. Spencer sold insurance and Mr. Burr had his office where he dealt in stamp collecting. This building has been altered today and houses Castiglione Jewelers.

This picture shows the corner of North Main and Middle Streets. The store on left of the picture is the Darling and Denton Store. Across Middle Street, the large building is Argersinger's Department Store. Remember the overhead conveyor that sent your money upstairs to the office and returned your change? Later this corner housed Woolworth's Store; today it is the sight of Ben Franklin. Argersinger's store is today an office complex.

The Getman Block on North Main Street was better known as the old Martin and Naylor's Department Store. This was Gloversville's other prominent department store. It, too, had a money exchange system with tubes and air that carried a cylinder in it so when you made a purchase, the money was placed inside the cylinder and your change was returned to you and the clerk. Today this building houses a number of stores.

The Martin and Naylor delivery wagon is shown here. The scene depicts the store south of its later place of business on North Main Street.

The Kasson Opera House or Memorial Hall, a four-story building with an impressive mansard roof, was built on the east side of North Main Street. It brought to Gloversville some of the city's earliest entertainment. Many famous entertainers performed here. Later, in the days of Vaudeville, it was called the Family Theater. It still remains an impressive structure on Main Street today.

This picture shows A.J. Kasson, early proprietor and founder of the Kasson Opera House (also known as Memorial Hall); with his assistant manager, W.R. Washburn; and his secretary, A.D. Bedford.

The interior of the old opera house, later the Family Theater, is shown here. Note the chandelier overhead with its many crystals. This was gas operated. If you arrived at the theater before the show, you could watch the lighting of these overhead lamps as the janitor, with a lighted torch on a long pole, rushed around the fixture before the room filled with gas.

This picture shows Mr. A.J. Kasson's residence on East Fulton Street, with all its gingerbread trim and the clock in the chimney. The garden and path in the back led to his horse stables and the rear entrance to his "Memorial Hall." Later this building was used as a boys club, and attached with a second-story overhead passageway to the YMCA, next door.

The east side of North Main Street is shown here. Mr. Kasson's home was built before he built the Kasson Villa on East Fulton Street. This building in later years was torn down and became the site of the Gloversville City Hall. Mr. Kasson, before building the opera house, owned and ran a glove shop south of this house. Note the old Gloversville Union Seminar to the left and back of the picture, later Gloversville High School.

In this similar view of the old Kasson home you can see in the background the city's first cemetery on the side of the hill. This was behind St. Mary's Church and the Fremont Street Methodist Church. Littauer Place is the hill in the background. Note the wooden tower with a bell, behind the Kasson home, which was part of the Congregational church on East Fulton Street. Earlier it had been used as the city fire bell.

The old city hall on Main Street is shown here with the bell tower and bell. The bell was sold for scrap during the war years. The fire department was housed to the left of the building. The building was built on the site of the old Kasson home, today used as the City Hall Restaurant.

A flash flood on Main Street rolls in front of the Kasson Opera House. City hall is to the left; note the Glove City lunch wagon and Hotel Germanie, up the street.

This view is looking down North Main Street the year Grover Cleveland was running for the presidency with Tom Hendrick as his running mate. Trees still grace Main Street. It looks like a milk delivery wagon is in the foreground.

Three

BLEECKER STREET SQUARE

This sketch was made looking up Bleecker Street from the square. The steeple of the Presbyterian church is in the background on West Fulton Street corner. The old Scoville House (hotel) is to the right in the foreground; this was a busy section of the city in its heyday. This sketch was drawn in October of 1879.

This is an early view of Bleecker Street Square before the First Methodist Church was built here. Bleecker Street runs north to the left of the photo. The large structure on the hill with the long columns is the old Captain Spaulding's Home. The front yard came down to the corner of Elm and Bleecker Streets. Captain Spaulding used to drill his local soldiers here. Today this is the site of the First Methodist Church.

Captain David Spaulding served in the Civil War. After the war the local GAR post raised money for a grave marker for Captain Spaulding in Prospect Hill Cemetery. Captain Spaulding, before the war, engaged in selling the new sewing machines.

This low wooden structure occupied the square on the northwest corner of Church and Bleecker Streets. Will Rupert's flour and feed store, the Blue Store (a grocery and meat market run by Mr. Sweet), and the Central Market were located here.

This is an artist's interpretation of the structure on fire, December 1883. The sketch shows a small dwelling on the corner. Note the firemen's hose cart in the foreground. An early Gloversville Fire Department hose cart has been preserved and is housed in the Fulton County Museum on Kingsboro Avenue.

The wooden structure on the southwest corner of Church and Bleecker Streets is shown here. This originally was called the Scoville House (see this chapter's title page). Later it was refurbished and called the Burlington. When the Burlington was destroyed by fire, a brick hotel took its place, but that building later succumbed to fire as well.

Fire destroyed the Burlington Hotel on Bleecker Street Square, October 2, 1891. Today this site is occupied by the Gloversville YWCA and the Senior Citizens Service Center of Gloversville and Fulton County. Note the old hose cart again in the foreground.

✳✳*   *✳*   **24 BLEECKER ST.,**   *   **GLOVERSVILLE, N. Y.**

This view was taken looking down Bleecker Street into Bleecker Street Square; the large impressive First Methodist Church now occupies the square. Note the drinking trough for horses in front of the church. To the right of the picture are the New York Lunch, Nicholson's Tavern, and Leonen's Meat Market. Upstairs was the New York State Unemployment Office. Mr C.H. Ayres ran a livery stable in back.

This is a later view of the First Methodist Church in Bleecker Street Square. The clock still remains in the tower, although the steeple has been changed and the drinking trough for horses has been replaced with a bandstand. Today a small park occupies the site of the bandstand.

This picture shows laying the foundation of a portion of the First Methodist Church in Bleecker Street Square. The stone mason in white coveralls in the foreground with trowel in hand is Gottlieb Brown, one of the city's foremost stone masons.

This is an interior view of the First Methodist Church, Bleecker Street Square, with its choir. Today this church has been placed on the Registry of Historic Sites in the state of New York.

Structures on Bleecker Street are shown here being torn down for the city's urban renewal. Remember Seld's Bargainville? At one time it housed the Italian social club, Alpha Nova.

This view looks north down Bleecker Street from West Fulton Street. The Presbyterian church is on the corner, and the Chinese laundry is located in the next building. Originally, the old city newspaper, *The Standard*, was published here. Today, it is the site of Weiner's store.

This is an early residence on the northeast corner of West Fulton and Bleecker Streets. In later years it was occupied by Loveday's Bakery. Young delivery boys used to peddle their bakery goods early in the morning going up and down city streets shouting, "One a penny, two a penny, hot cross buns." Being competitive with one another caused them to start out earlier each morning, until it had to be stopped, as they were waking residents too early.

Governor Nelson Rockafellow emerges from a convertible in Bleecker Street Square. Lieutenant Loran Baker, from the Gloversville Police Department, is in the left of the picture in the foreground.

A parade in Bleecker Street Square is shown here. The Grand Union was then on the corner of Bleecker and Church Streets, where the YWCA is today. Note the buildings in the background, which were torn down for the city's urban renewal; today the site is a parking lot.

This view looks up Church Street from Bleecker Street Square. Senator's Restaurant, Pyne's Plumbing and Heating, the Coronet Photo Studio, and Mr. Blodgett's Cleaners can all be seen. On the other side of street was Chipper's Men and Boys Clothiers, Kingsbury Jewelers, Mr. Berger's Bakery, and, on the corner, Mr. Dence, the jeweler, just to name a few. Today, the left side and part of the opposite side of the street are a parking lot.

Elm Street is shown here, looking toward Bleecker Street Square. The white house second to the right was Dr. Robert Palmer's home. He served for over 40 years as county historian. The large brick building is the old Darling Theater.

Looking up Bleecker Street, a few doors past the Eighth Avenue intersection, the Adirondack Hotel and Bar can be seen. Mr. Ellis's gas station (Sinclair Gas) was a favorite stop coming and going to Bleecker.

Four

THE SOUTH END

An early road crew excavates the road bed for the new city street in front of the Baptist church on South Main Street.

This was once the oldest home in Gloversville. It occupied the site behind the present-day New York State Employment Office on South Main Street. Located next to the creek, it was known as the Livingston/Hulett home.

The Century Block, today the site of the New York State Employment Office, was located at 199 South Main Street.

The Trinity Chapel is located on South Main across from the Hill Street intersection. The steps in the sand bank are still evident today. Prior to the church, this was the site of an early one-room schoolhouse, built to service this end of the city.

Students attend the old one-room schoolhouse on South Main Street. This was later the site of the Trinity Church Chapel.

The old Alvord Hotel, on the corner where South Main intersects with Cayadutta Street, is shown here. This was one of the city's finest hotels until it was destroyed in a fire that killed several people. Note the water trough next to the fire hydrant on the corner.

This is an artist's rendition of the Alvord Hotel on South Main Street. Note the mineral springs house to the left of the picture. You could, at one time, obtain bottled mineral waters from the spring, which was located on the bank of Cayadutta Creek. The Hotel Billiard Rooms and Vine Street are to the right.

In later years, after the fire, the Gloversville Post Office was built on the site of the old Alvord Hotel on South Main Street. Note the drinking trough for horses which was still visible next to the fire hydrant. Later this post office was torn down and a new one built on North Main Street, where it remains today.

Mr. Davis ran a livery stable, just below the old Alvord House on Forest Street, which was connected with the hotel. Mr. Davis did not believe the new automobile would take the place of his livery stable, as he is demonstrating here in front of his business, but eventually even Mr. Davis would succumb to the new mode of transportation.

This 1891 photograph shows the old Keystone Hotel on the corner of Washington and South Main Street. Today the law offices of Attorney Mario Albanese are located here.

This is a later view of the Keystone Hotel and Bar, with a brick section built on the Washington Street side (later this was a newsroom). This structure burned down and was replaced by a brick edifice.

A brick building was built on the site of the old Keystone Hotel. In later years it housed Steve's Tavern and one of Gloversville's first Stewart shops with their "make your own sundae."

The south end was plagued by a number of fires through the years. Here is a view of the Teetz Block disaster at 46–48 South Main Street. This occurred on April 16, 1895. Two were killed and four were injured in the incident. Those in the photograph are "searching for bodies."

For years, the Kingsboro Hotel was the city's most impressive hotel. It featured a banquet hall, ballroom, and a tavern in the basement. Here, the old marquee is shown stretching across the sidewalk on South Main Street at the hotel entrance.

This is a winter view of South Main Street, in front of the Kingsboro Hotel. Note the trolley tracks are plowed and the snow banks on each side are used for horse-drawn sleighs.

This is an interior view of the main dining room of the Kingsboro Hotel. Today this hotel, located on South Main Street, has been turned into the Kingsboro Apartments.

This is another interior view of the Kingsboro Hotel, showing the lobby and the office.

South Main Street is shown here. To the left of the picture are the tall white pillars of a house. This home had the city's first white marble sidewalk in front of it. It is located just south of the Kingsboro Hotel.

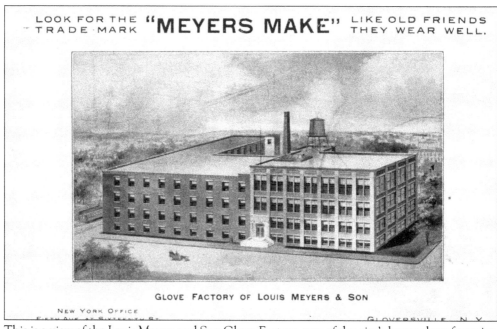

LOOK FOR THE "MEYERS MAKE" LIKE OLD FRIENDS
TRADE-MARK THEY WEAR WELL.

GLOVE FACTORY OF LOUIS MEYERS & SON

NEW YORK OFFICE
GLOVERSVILLE N. Y.

This is a view of the Louis Meyers and Son Glove Factory, one of the city's larger glove factories, located on West Pine Street, next to the railroad tracks.

The back of the Littauer Brothers Glove Factory, off South Main Street, is shown here. The workers are along the railroad north of Pine Street Crossing. After attending Harvard University, Lucius Littauer returned home to Gloversville to run the factory. Later he became our congressman from this district.

This is the old Churchill home on South Main Street, south of East Pine Street, near the present-day site of the St. Mary's, Mount Carmel School. It was said to have had the first indoor bathroom in the village. It was built of three walls; the outside was wood, the middle was brick, and inner wall was lathe and plaster. It had sliding inside blinds on all downstairs windows and the dining room was built as an octagon.

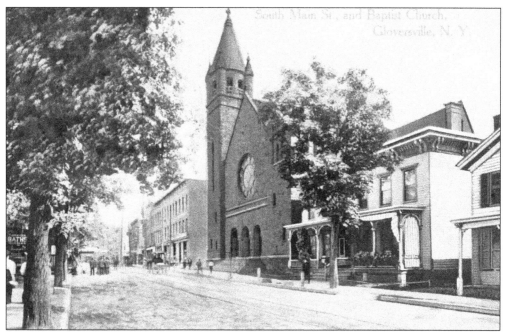

The Baptist church on South Main Street is shown here. This is the second church on this site; the original church was destroyed by fire. Next door, to the south of the church, was later Del Negro's Pharmacy, now the parking lot of H.P. Motor's.

This is an interior view of the old Baptist church on South Main Street, Gloversville.

The old Fonda home on South Main Street, with its gingerbread decor, is shown here. The Fonda sisters lived here until it was torn down. It was located on the lot where Sarrino Brother and Curcio Inc. sold wholesale fruits and beverages.

Mr. and Mrs. Zimmer pose in a horse-drawn cutter in front of Stewart Wilson's Photograph Studio. (Mr. Wilson later became known as the "Sacandaga Hermit.") The studio was located on South Main Street, south of Hill Street, where today is located Clemente Latham Concrete. Mr. Zimmer resided on South Main below Harrison Street.

Mr. and Mrs. Zimmer advertise for their hound dogs and game chickens (raised for show). Mr Zimmer was a noted raiser of "Beagle" hunting dogs. He used to walk his cow and horse down Harrison Street to pasture.

One of the city's lunch wagons, adapted from an old railroad car, was located at 72 1/2 South Main Street. These lunch wagons became quite popular throughout the city in the early 1900s. The proprietor at this location was Leslie Conar.

Five

THE NORTH END

The Veterans Memorial in the square at the intersection of North Main Street and Eight Avenue, in our city's north end, depicts Union Civil War soldiers. The bayonets were removed in later years for safety.

One of Gloversville's early glove factories was located on Glove Street, a short, dead-end street off East State Street. Only one building remains today.

The old Heacock home was located on the corner of North Main and State Streets. This was the original site of the second school in the Kingsboro section of the city. The school was moved to the opposite southeast corner when this home was built.

This is the one-time Gloversville Business School on East State Street. Originally the old Judson Estate, today it is the location of The Getman Memorial Home.

Here is an early advertisement for the Gloversville Business School.

This view looks up North Main Street from the Eighth Avenue intersection. The small brick building in the square, part of the Gloversville/Kingsboro Water Works, was used to monitor and regulate the water. Later this building was removed and the war memorial was placed in this square (see this chapter's title page).

A parade on North Main and the dedication of the war memorial in the square are shown here.

A World War I parade is shown here at the intersection of Eighth Avenue and North Main Street. Members of the city's Elk's Club carry their large American flag. Note the Columbia School to the right of the photo.

This is a view of the old Columbia School on the southwest corner of Eighth Avenue and North Main Street. Mrs. Thompson and Myrtle Hobbs taught here. Mrs. Topliff served at one time as principal. Today it has been altered into apartments for housing.

The North Main Street M.E. Church is shown here on the corner of Seventh Avenue and North Main Street. The first church was a wooden structure. The pastor's house is to the left of the church. This is across from the old Columbia School.

This old wooden structure at 223 North Main was later replaced with a brick building located south of Quigley's Bar, on the same side of North Main Street.

How many remember the old Moose Lodge, next to the corner of First Avenue and North Main Street, with Saturday night dances and the one-armed bandits in its basement? Today it occupies a site over the city line on the extension of East State Street.

The old Marshall home is located on the corner of Third Avenue and North Main Street. Third Avenue was once called Marshall Avenue. This house was left to the city for use as a museum, but it was later was converted into the Third Avenue Fire Station.

The Marshall home, after being converted into one of the city's fire stations, is used today by the Gloversville Water Works. The building to the right of the picture and up Third Avenue was the home of Professor Estee (for whom the city's middle school was named).

This old home was located on North Main Street, across from Fourth Avenue. It was torn down and later a grocery store was built here (the old Acme Market). Today an auto parts dealer, Lamie's Auto Supply, occupies this site.

This view shows the early headquarters of the Gloversville YWCA, then located on Spring Street, where the park is next to the Salvation Army Chapel. There was no street or road cut out here at that time. Today the YWCA operates out of the large brick structure in Bleecker Street Square.

The Spring Street Apartments are shown here during a fire. They were located on Spring Street, across from the Elm Street intersection. This was before Elm Street was extended; today this location takes in part of the park and the new street. You can see the Salvation Army Chapel to the right of the photo.

This is the old Penny Giles house being moved from its original location on the northwest corner of North Main and Middle Streets, making room for the new Argersinger Building. This old house was moved a couple doors up the street on North Main, where it remained one of the oldest structures on Main Street until it was torn down by the City to make room for a parking lot.

This is a view of the old Gloversville Union Seminar on the lot at the corners of Prospect Avenue and North Main Street. This site later became the Gloversville High School and part of Estee Middle School. Recently a new school has been built on top of Lincoln Street Hill, where both complexes are housed today.

This is an early winter scene of the old academy, with A.D. Kibbe, Winsor Hotel hack, in front. In the background can be seen both the north and south buildings on each side of the old academy. The south building was torn down for Estee School. The north building remained for a number of years when it was used by the band. Glove sewing was also taught here.

Students form a human flag, comprised of seven hundred children, for the 1915 Fourth of July celebration. The new tapestry-brick high school building in the back ground took the place of the old red-bricked academy building.

The 1898 Fourth of July celebration is shown here in front of the old Union Seminar. This was the year the Spanish-American War began.

One of Gloversville's early school football squads is shown here lined up by the side of the old north building. Some of students are identified as Long, W. Eichile, Woram, Almy, Foltz, Mandulan, C. Hatch, Van Buren, Layton, and F. Hatch.

Professor Platt poses with his teaching staff at the old Gloversville Union Seminar, later Gloversville High School. Professor Pratt has been credited with finding the first potato bug that came to town.

This is the interior of the old Gloversville High School auditorium. The building was later used as the city's school administration building.

This life-size bronze statue was erected in honor of Lucius Littauer. Born to immigrant parents in Gloversville, he studied at Harvard University, returning to Gloversville to engage in his father's glove-manufacturing business. He eventually became our congressman and was a personal friend and advisor to Teddy Roosevelt, governor and later president of the United States. Lucius became a city benefactor. He was very successful, and shared his wealth with his hometown.

Lucius Littauer, in center of this photo with the white moustache, is being greeted on the platform at the dedication of his life-size bronze statue. The statue of one of Gloversville's greatest benefactors still graces the corner of Prospect Avenue and North Main Street.

Six

VANISHING SCENES

Gloversville had the reputation of being a circus town. Many major circuses and Wild West shows included Gloversville on their tours, as it could be readily accessed by rail. Elephants are seen here turning up East Fulton Street at the Four Corners. Note the large crowds then, even in a rain shower.

The circus trains unloaded on West Fulton Street and the wagons and animals were led off to the circus lot in the city. With a preview of what to expect, a parade was led up Main Street.

Crowds turned out for the circus parades. This scene is at the Four Corners with elephants being led up Main Street.

Elephants were a favorite to photograph. This scene was taken on the corner of Church and North Main Streets, where Martin & Naylor was established before moving to the larger department store up the street. Today Key Bank is located here.

This remains one of the author's favorite pictures, as it shows the elephants sauntering up Bleecker Street in front of his home at 187 Bleecker Street. Note the children following along by the elephants.

This is an 1893 view of the Barnum and Bailey Circus in Gloversville. The famous Jumbo came to Gloversville with the Barnum and Bailey Circus shortly before the much-loved elephant met its fate in a train accident in Canada.

In between the circuses came the Wild West shows. Here was advertised "Pawnee Bill's Wild West Show" coming to Gloversville.

The 101 Wild West Show parade is shown here coming down Bleecker Street in 1913, with cowboys and a stagecoach following.

This is another view of the parade on Bleecker Street, with Native Americans following in full headdress. The Hotel Charles is in the center of the photograph. Mr. Bramer, "The Stove Man," was located in the area where the Gloversville Sports Shop is today.

It was a big day to youngsters when "Buffalo Bill" came to town with his show. My father used to recall as a young boy having had the privilege of meeting him and shaking his hand.

The last circus parade in Gloversville took place on August 13, 1953. This picture shows the band wagon of King Brothers, Cristians Combined Circus, on its way up East Fulton in front of the *Leader Herald* newspaper headquarters. This circus had 12 elephants.

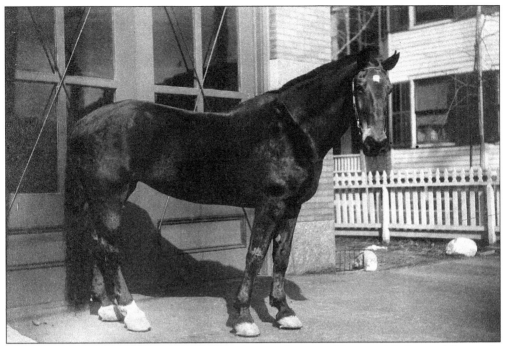

Kit, the last fire department horse to be retired, was a favorite of the city. Mechanized fire trucks pushed Kit aside but he was always remembered for his dedication.

Kit is shown here in action, turning up Washington Street after rounding the corner of South Main Street. He was finally put to pasture as a devoted public servant.

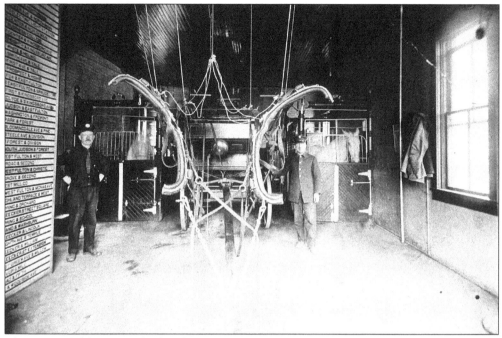

This suspended harness is displayed at the North Main Street Fire House. It enabled the horses, seen in the stalls in the background, to be harnessed quickly, so that the wagon could be all hooked up and ready to go in no time.

This view shows the North Main Fire Station, built in 1902, with the team of white horses harnessed to the wagon and ready to go. Today the city has one central fire station and dispatch on Frontage Road, next to the new city hall.

This is an early view of the Gloversville Fire Department's hook and ladder, all decked out for a parade on Main Street.

A traveling harpist and a three-piece orchestra provide entertainment on Main Street. Traveling entertainers—including organ grinders with their monkeys, acrobats, and musicians—frequented the city.

Here, "Captain Baldwin's Red Devil," an early air show, is advertised as coming to Gloversville. Fireworks, parades, and hot-air balloon ascensions were included in the city's early Fourth of July celebration.

James Barr was appointed the first policeman in Gloversville on May 18, 1857. Gloversville's first lock-up (or jail), was on Gas Alley, behind the present-day Baptist church of South Main Street. Officer Barr, when Gloversville became a dry village, ran his own private drinking oasis across the city line in Stockmore's Clearing.

There used to be a police officer assigned to the Four Corners to assist the flow of traffic and provide a presence on Main Street. In later years he was afforded a small shelter to get out of the elements and for communication. Here we see one of the early officers of the Four Corners, conferring with a local pedestrian.

Baseball, the all-American sport, struck Gloversville at an early stage when a semi-pro team and league was formed. The Gloversville Baseball Park was established on the extension of Fifth Avenue, where Wal Mart and Hannaford Foods are today.

This photograph was taken in the bleachers, looking out on the diamond. The team, "The Glovers," was headquartered here. The field was used for other special events as well as boxing and shows.

The Glovers took on the Schenectady Blue Jays, the Amsterdam Rug Beaters, and Three Rivers, to name a few. This old ball club turned out some great players and games.

Gloversville produced a number of local bands and orchestras that played on special occasions and at local opera houses and theaters. Here is the Gloversville Military Band, who would shortly depart to play a summer concert at Sacandaga Park, "The Coney Island of the North."

Gloversville boasted several houses of entertainment—the old Kasson Opera House (later the Family Theater), and in more recent years, the Glove and Hippodrome Movie Theaters. On Elm Street, across from Middle Street, was the Darling Theater. The third floor once housed a movie studio called the Blaze Studio; in later years the second floor served as a bowling alley.

FRANK THOMPSON
PRESENTS DENMAN THOMPSON'S
"THE OLD HOMESTEAD"
Hear the Famous Double Quartet   See the Beautiful Church Scene
Full Scenic Production   SEATS NOW ON SALE
DARLING Theatre
Gloversville
New Year's Day and Night, JAN.

THAT'S THE SWANZEY BAND THINK THEY'RE GOING TO HAVE ICE CREAM

Many early entertainers performed in "the old Darling." When the popular play *Uncle Tom's Cabin* came to town, a parade proceeded down Main Street as advertisement for the play in the Darling Theater. Large Great Danes were led down Main Street on heavy leads, in pursuit of "Little Eva." Here is an advertisement of an up-and-coming show at the Darling.

DARLING THEATRE

THURSDAY, MAY 12 - 1910

LILLIAN RUSSELL

—IN—

THE FIRST NIGHT

By GEO. V HOBART

(Adapted from "Der halbe Dichter" by Rosen. The same
German source as "Nancy & Co." by Augustin Daly.)
Stage Direction of Lawrence Marston.

CHARACTERS.

Colonel Ketchum, a particular papa...........Digby Bell
Jessie, his daughter ....Mary Faber
Mabel, his other daughter.............Leonora Oaksford
Mrs. Pfitzer, his sister ....Susanne Westford
Langdon Jones, an author ....Richard Thornton
Mortimer Smith, a lawyer ....Sydney Booth
Murgatroyd Howe, a young man with money.Geo. E. Mack
Jerry Graham ....Frederick Truesdell
Luke Sharp, a chauffeur ....Hayes Hunter
Entington, a waiter ....Frank L. Jones
Mina, a maid ....Saidee Williams
and
Rose Graham ....Lillian Russell

SYNOPSIS.

ACT I.—Reception hall in Colonel Ketchum's residence
in the suburbs of New York.
TIME—Monday noon.
ACT II.—A private parlor in the Astoregis Hotel, New
York City.
TIME—Monday afternoon.
ACT III.—Same as Act I.
TIME—Monday night.

Many early notable actresses and actors appeared in the city's local theaters. Advertised here, in a 1910 flyer, is Lillian Russell to appear on stage at the Darling. Lillian was a favorite of "Diamond Jim Brady."

This flyer advertises the Schine's Theaters in Gloversville. The Glove, the Schine's flagship theater, is featuring *Bringing Up Father in Ireland*, while the Hippodrome, on East Fulton Street, is showing *The Covered Wagon*.

The Odd Fellows Temple, on East Fulton Street, was later converted into The Hippodrome Movie Theater. Its front entrance was altered to have a marquee over the street. Later this structure was demolished and today this site is part of the new Knesseth Israel Synagogue on the corner of Fremont and East Fulton Streets.

One of Gloversville's most unique outdoor sculptures is *The Thinking Doughboy*, which has for years graced the front entrance to the city's old high school on North Main Street. This colossal bronze statue, depicting a World War I G.I. holding a German helmet in his hands, seems to ponder, "Why?" It was placed here after "the war to end all wars," and is certainly different from other war memorials.

These "cadets" are really a city youth group formed as a drill team. They were housed in the basement of the First M.E. Church in Bleecker Street Square, and were drilled by an old veteran. Many of these young men later went off to fight in the First World War. The author's father, Gordon L. Decker, is the young lad in the second row, second cadet in from the right, who is turned toward the camera. He later served in France.

Gloversville maintains a number of public parks, and a new one was recently installed off West Fulton Street at the site of the old F.J. & G. R.R. headquarters. Located on the hill overlooking the city is Meyers Park, one of its most impressive parks, with its walking trails, flowers, shrubs, and its old bandstand.

Melchoir Park on Kingsboro Avenue, laid out from an old race track, is one of the city's most beautiful parks. This old drinking fountain has disappeared today. The park shelters one of the city's Civil War monuments. Evening band concerts are often held here.

107

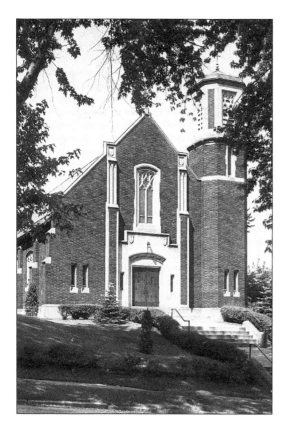

The Gloversville city skyline is silhouetted with many of its church steeples and houses of worship. This was St. Francis of De Sales on West Pine Street, a Catholic church comprised primarily of early German families, which ran and maintained a Catholic school on its grounds. The original wooden church on this site was built as an Episcopal church. Today this church is privately owned.

The St. Francis Catholic School on East Third Street is no longer used today as a school. One of the school classes poses for a photograph in the side yard (the author is in this group shot).

St. Mary's Catholic Church was located on Fremont Street. It has succumb to consolidation, merging with Mount Carmel Church on South Main Street today. In the past, St. Mary's maintained a school; today this school is used as a county office complex on East Fulton Street. The one-story brick building to the left of the church was the Nuns Home. Pictured here as well is the Fremont Methodist Church.

This was the interior of the St. Mary's Catholic Church on Fremont Street. Today the site is a vacant lot. Gone are the beautiful arched ceilings and white marble altar.

Another place of worship on Kingsboro Avenue was the First Church of Christian Science. It maintained a reading room on Spring Street, just off North Main. Today this church has been sold and is privately owned.

The Gloversville Congregational Church on East Fulton Street went through a number of changes through the years. The tower of the church remains separated from the rest of the church to this day. The first church on this site also had a separate tower (of wood) which sat in the back and to the side of the present church.

The old wooden bell tower of the East Fulton Street Congregational Church is shown here. Until the city procured its own fire bell in the tower of old city hall, this bell was used as a fire alarm in the city.

The old Jewish synagogue was located on East Fulton Street. This site today takes in part of the basketball court and park on the corner of East Fulton and Market Streets. The short street to the left of the temple was called Elk Lane. Today a new synagogue takes its place south of here on East Fulton and the corner of Fremont Street.

St. James Lutheran Church is shown here when it occupied the corner lot of Grand and Hamilton Streets. Today this church has been rebuilt out on the extension of North Main. On this site today is located the dental office of Dr. Stephen Freeman.

This is a view of the old A.M.E. Zion Church at the corner of Chestnut and East Fulton Streets. Destroyed by fire, it was rebuilt on this same site and is still serving the community today.

This is an early view looking down Fremont Street. The Fremont Methodist Church is in the background. The houses to the left of the photo are where Estee Middle School was constructed.

This old tavern was located on East Fulton Street, across from Chestnut Street. In later years it was know as Woodleys Tavern. Today Leonzo Pizza Parlor occupies this location.

The old Nathan Littauer Hospital was located on Prospect Place, overlooking the city. It afforded the citizens of Gloversville the finest care in its day. The long, enclosed walkway to the left of the picture led to the Nurses Home and School. Today a new and modern hospital has been built off East State Street.

A group of nurses from the old Littauer School of Nursing are shown here, all capped and ready to serve.

The Gloversville Free Library on the southeast corner of East Fulton and Fremont Streets is a most impressive structure. Built as a Carnegie library, it is maintained with a reading room, lending library, and a history and genealogy room.

The Gloversville Library is shown here under construction. Gottlieb Brown (one of Gloversville's stone masons) appears at the base of the column in his white mason coveralls with the contractor, Mr. A.E. Brace.

The office of the *Leader Republican* newspaper was located on East Fulton Street, near the Four Corners. This has been for years our county and city newspaper; today it is called the *Leader Herald*. Note the headliner on the inside front window which gave you up-to-date happenings from over the ticker tape.

W.B. Dodge, an 1890 newspaper boy, delivers an Albany paper in Gloversville. Several newspapers found their home here through the years. Today the *Leader Herald* remains and has home delivery with a staff of delivery personnel throughout the city.

Seba Fry resided on Fruit Street. He ran a store on Main Street, West Fulton Street, and later on Bleecker Street. He sold groceries and delivered with his delivery wagon, pictured here. At one time he had a pawn shop and sold Hupmobile cars.

Seba Fry's advertising flyer is pictured here.

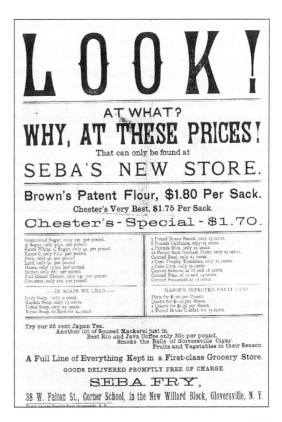

LOOK!

AT WHAT?
WHY, AT THESE PRICES!
That can only be found at

SEBA'S NEW STORE.

Brown's Patent Flour, $1.80 Per Sack.
Chester's Very Best, $1.75 Per Sack.
Chester's - Special - $1.70.

Granulated Sugar, only 10c. per pound.
A Sugar, only 9½c. per pound
Extra White, C Sugar, only 9c. per pound
Extra C, only 8½c. per pound.
Pork, only 9c. per pound.
Lard, only 9c. per pound.
Hams, only 13½c. per pound.
Butter, only 22c. per pound.
Full Cream Cheese, only 14c. per pound.
Cocoanut, only 25c. per pound.

3 Pound Boxes Starch, only 23 cents.
6 Pounds Oatflakes, only 25 cents.
4 Pounds Rice, only 25 cents.
10 Pound Sack Graham Flour, only 35 cents.
Canned Beef, only 23 cents.
3 Cans Trophy Tomatoes, only 25 cents.
4 Cans Corn, only 25 cents.
Canned Salmon, at 16 and 18 cents.
Canned Peas, at 10 and 14 cents.
Canned Succotash at 13 cents.

——IN SOAPS WE LEAD.——

Ivory Soap, only 9 cents.
Napkin Soap, only 23 cents.
Towel Soap, only 23 cents.
Novel Soap, 10 Bars for 24 cents.

MASON'S IMPROVED FRUIT CANS

Pints for $1.00 per Dozen.
Quarts for $1.10 per dozen.
2 Quarts for $1.35 per dozen.
2 Pound Bricks Codfish for 15 cents.

Try our 25 cent Japan Tea.
Another lot of Soused Mackerel just in.
Best Rio and Java Coffee only 30c per pound.
Smoke the Belle of Gloversville Cigar.
Fruits and Vegetables in their Season.

A Full Line of Everything Kept in a First-class Grocery Store.
GOODS DELIVERED PROMPTLY FREE OF CHARGE.

SEBA FRY,
38 W. Fulton St., Corner School, in the New Willard Block, Gloversville, N. Y.

The old Palmer House, an early boarding house, was located on the top of Cayadutta Street Hill on the east side of the street, where a parking lot is today.

This business card describes the Palmer House.

This is a view of the Gloversville Armory on Washington Street. Many of our local boys left here for the battlefields of France during the First World War, and for the South Pacific during World War II. The armory has been a local center for shows, dances, and civic functions as well.

This is a view of Feldman's Bakery on Washington Street, now Rauch and Son Bakery, known for their hard rolls. Mr. Farhart used to sell Buick automobiles next door, on what is now the site of One Shot Deal and Glen's Tavern.

How many readers remember Polly's diner on 141 North Main Street? There were a number of restaurants and lunch wagons where you could get a good BLT or a western egg. This was before all the pizza parlors.

This is a view of the old Place home that stood on the corner of West Fulton and South Arlington Avenue, where the telephone building was located for years. Arlington Avenue was once called School Street, named after the third school in the city, on the northwest corner of what is today North Arlington Avenue and West Fulton Street.

This is a view of the old Adler Glove Factory on the corner of Forest and Park Streets. At one time, you could find a glove shop or business allied to it on most every street in the city. Gloversville was the Glove Capital of the nation, if not the world, in its heyday.

The old Berry and Allen Glove Factory was located on the corner of Cayadutta and West Fulton. The company ran a grocery store in the basement where the workers could be paid in scrip, good at the store, or run up credit until payday (remember the old song, "I Owe My Soul To the Company Store?"). The building is still standing but is no longer a glove shop. It is shown here c. 1880–81.

Glove cutters had a special dress code at work, and sported long-sleeved white shirts and ties, a trade distinction. Many of our city's immigrants came to Gloversville as glove cutters, a trade usually handed down from father to son. One of Gloversville's early labor disputes was with the glove cutters.

These workers were employed by St. Thomas, Inc. Besides gloves, some factories turned out leather accessories such as wallets, purses, and eyeglass cases.

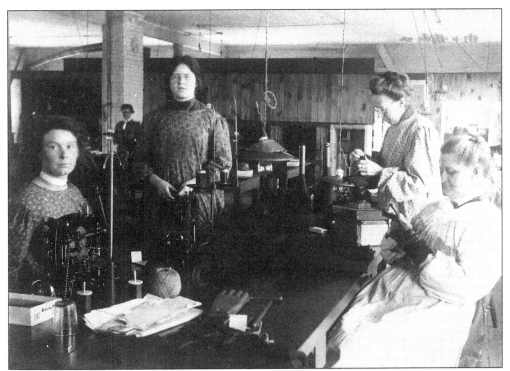

This is an interior view of a glove shop. It was advertised that in Gloversville a fellow could always find an industrious wife. A woman who had some experience in sewing could usually find a job in one of the glove shops. Some specialized in certain types of glove making.

These glove makers worked in one of the city's many glove shops. Just about every street had a glove shop, leather mill, or some allied business connected with the trade. Each lady had her own chair, table, and sewing machine, and usually was paid by the piece.

The Gloversville School System taught glove making for years as part of the vocational school. Many young ladies were taught the trade by skilled glove makers, thus producing a steady workforce for the local manufacturers. Today, most of the gloves are manufactured outside the U.S. and imported. Now only a few local manufacturers actually make the gloves here.

The Gloversville Knitting Mill was located on Beaver Street. Many businesses were allied with the glove and leather industry, including the silk mill, teamsters, tool and dye makers, the hair mill on Harrison Street, the glue factory, and the box and paper manufactures, just to name a few. Cloth linings were used in mittens and gloves.

The old Starr and Geisler Leather Mill was located north off Harrison Street, along the Cayadutta Creek (behind what is today Taylor Made Products Inc., on the Arterial Highway, Route 30A).

The Martin and Deichsel Leather Mill in the south end, north off Harrison Street, met its fate by fire. This was previously the old Starr Mill.

Leather workers engage in the processing of leather. Leather processing went through a number of stages. The dried, raw hides were first soaked in vats, and were then shaved, dyed and colored, bucktailed, split, measured, and graded. They then went from wet room to dry room until the leather was ready to be used in fine gloves, leather accessories, and shoes.

The Kent and Company Leather Mill, later known as Booth and Kent and Company, was a large leather mill operation on Washburn and Grand Streets, across from Kent Street. It used to close its doors on special occasions and holidays, sometimes leasing several railroad cars for its employees to go to Sacandaga Park with their families.

These leather workers were photographed inside one of the city's many leather mills. It looks like a coloring department, with finished hides stacked on horses.

G. Levor & Mills Brothers Leather Factories, Gloversville, N. Y.

Shown here are Gus Levor's Leather Mill and the Mills Brothers Leather Factory (to the right of the picture). Both of these were located off West Fulton Street. Gus Levor started off as a rag dealer and peddler. Levor's mill became one of the city's largest.

Leather workers from Levor's mill pose for a group shot. Work could usually be found for experienced workers even during the Depression. Leather products were always in demand (especially during the war years, for the military) and were protected with a high tariff.

1885 1935

PLANTED FOREST
GLOVERSVILLE CITY FOREST,
THE FIRST ESTABLISHED WITH
STATE PLANTING STOCK,
BETWEEN 1909 AND 1935
743,000 TREES WERE PLANTED.
NEW YORK STATE EDUCATION AND
CONSERVATION DEPARTMENTS. 1935

This historic marker was placed on the Gloversville Water Works property, on the extension of Easterly Street. It was re-dedicated recently by the commissioner at that time, Henry Williams of the New York Department of Environmental Conservation, along with Mayor Susan Hammond.

Printed in the USA
CPSIA information can be obtained
at www.ICGtesting.com
LVHW081957171123
764248LV00009B/840